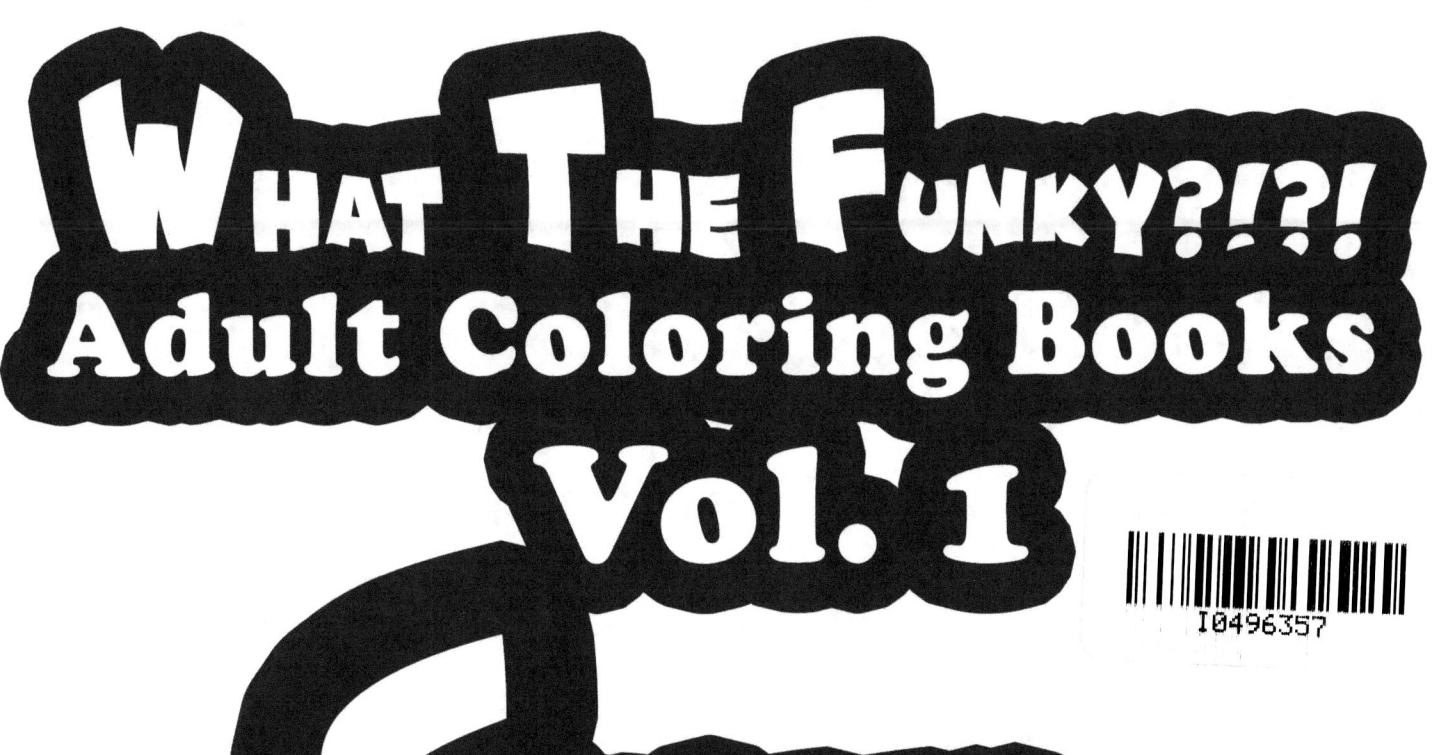

ADD US ON SOCIAL MEDIA!
Instagram: @WhatTheFunkyACB
Twitter: @WhatTheFunkyACB
Facebook: @WhatTheFunkyACB
Email: whatthefunky3000@gmail.com
Copyright 2021

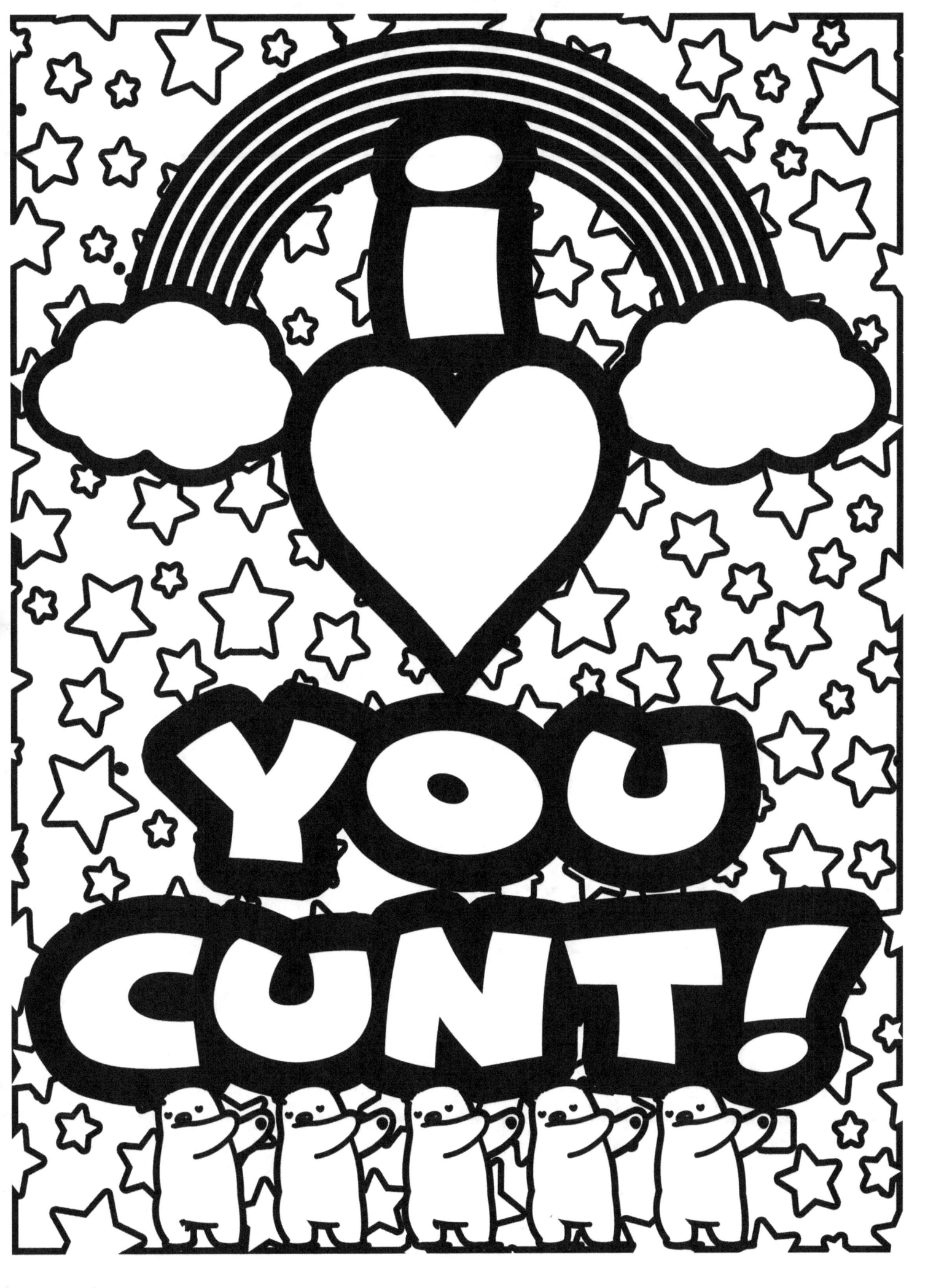

YOU'RE THE BEST PIECE OF i KNOW!!!

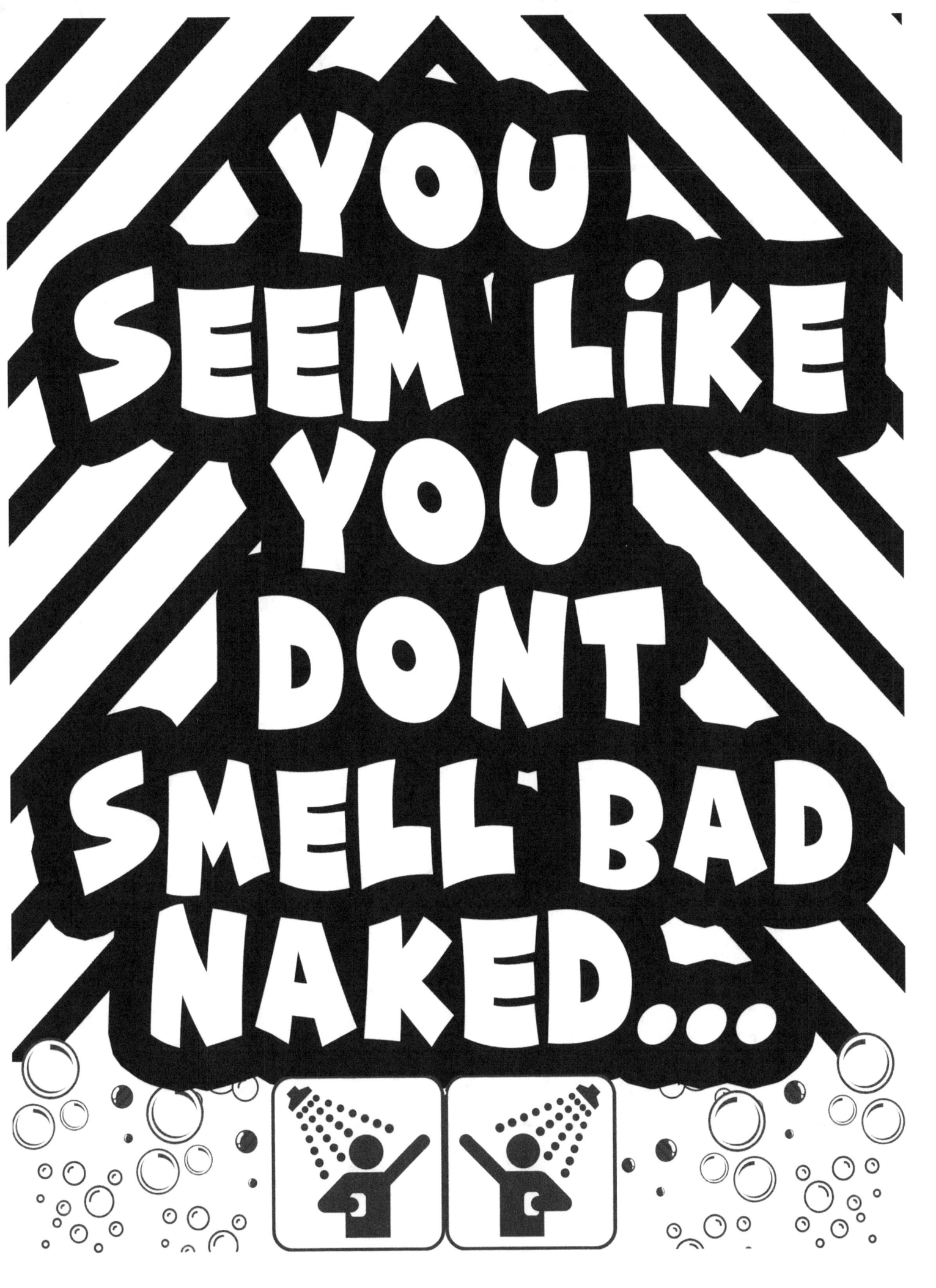

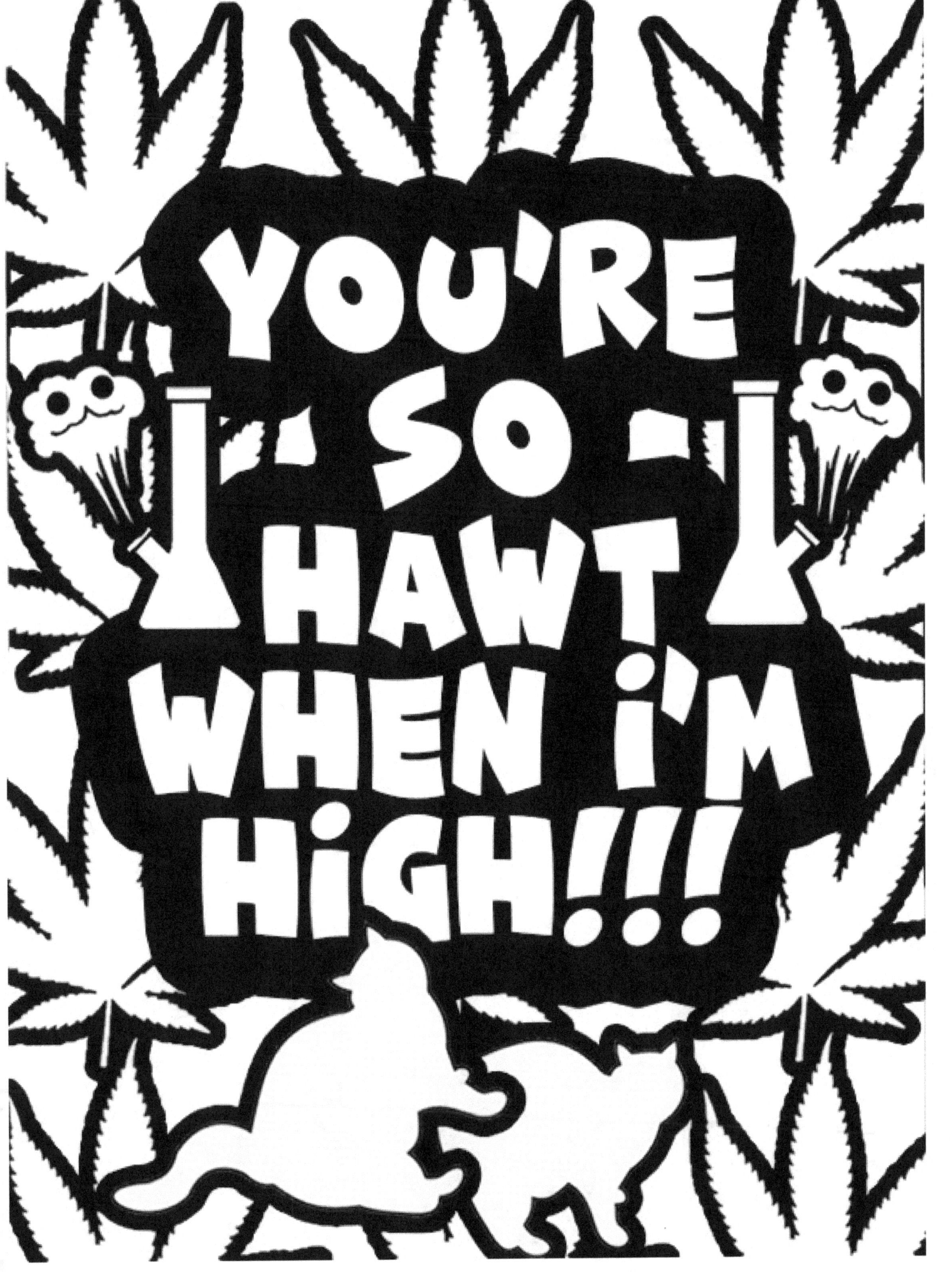

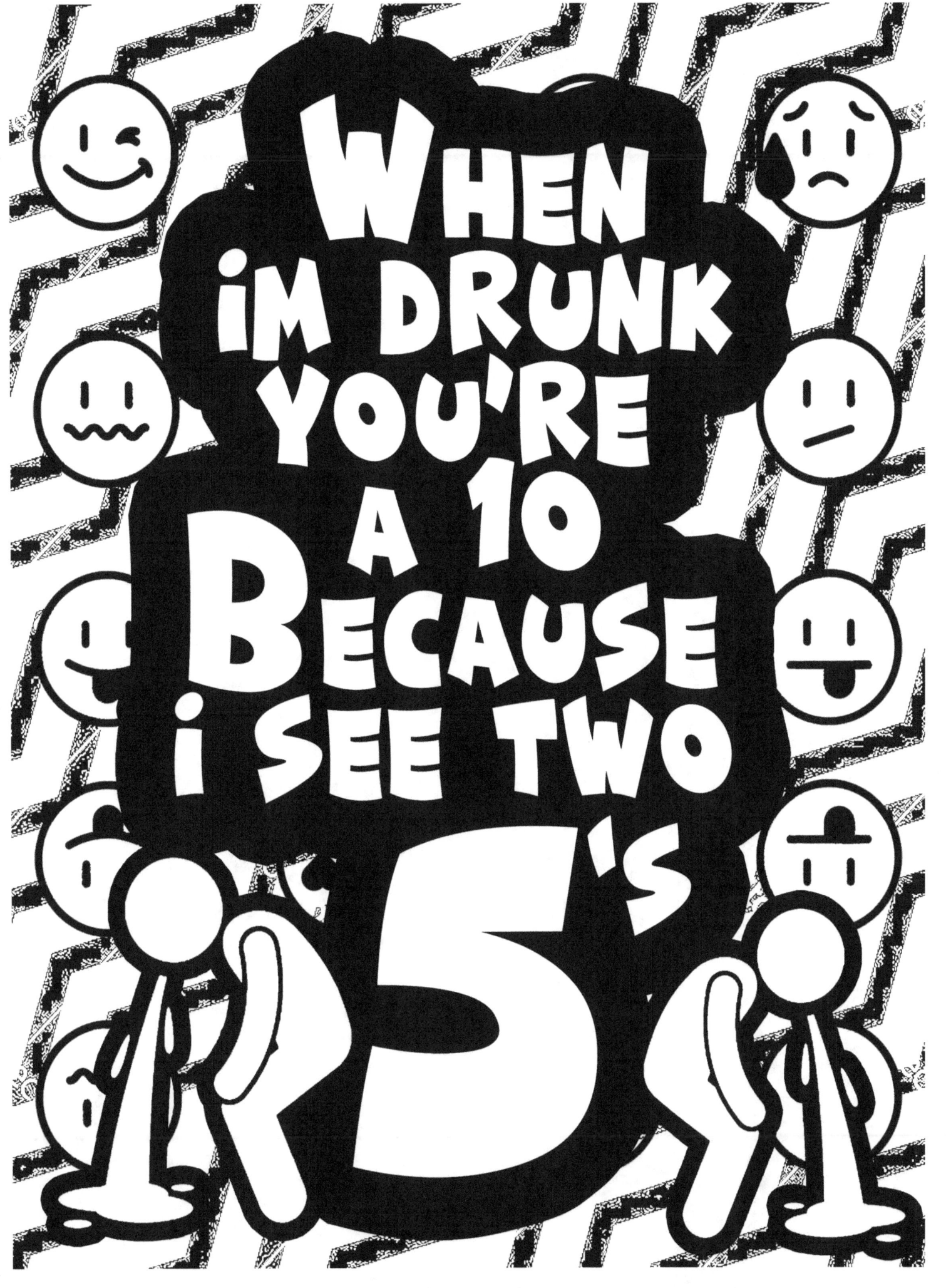

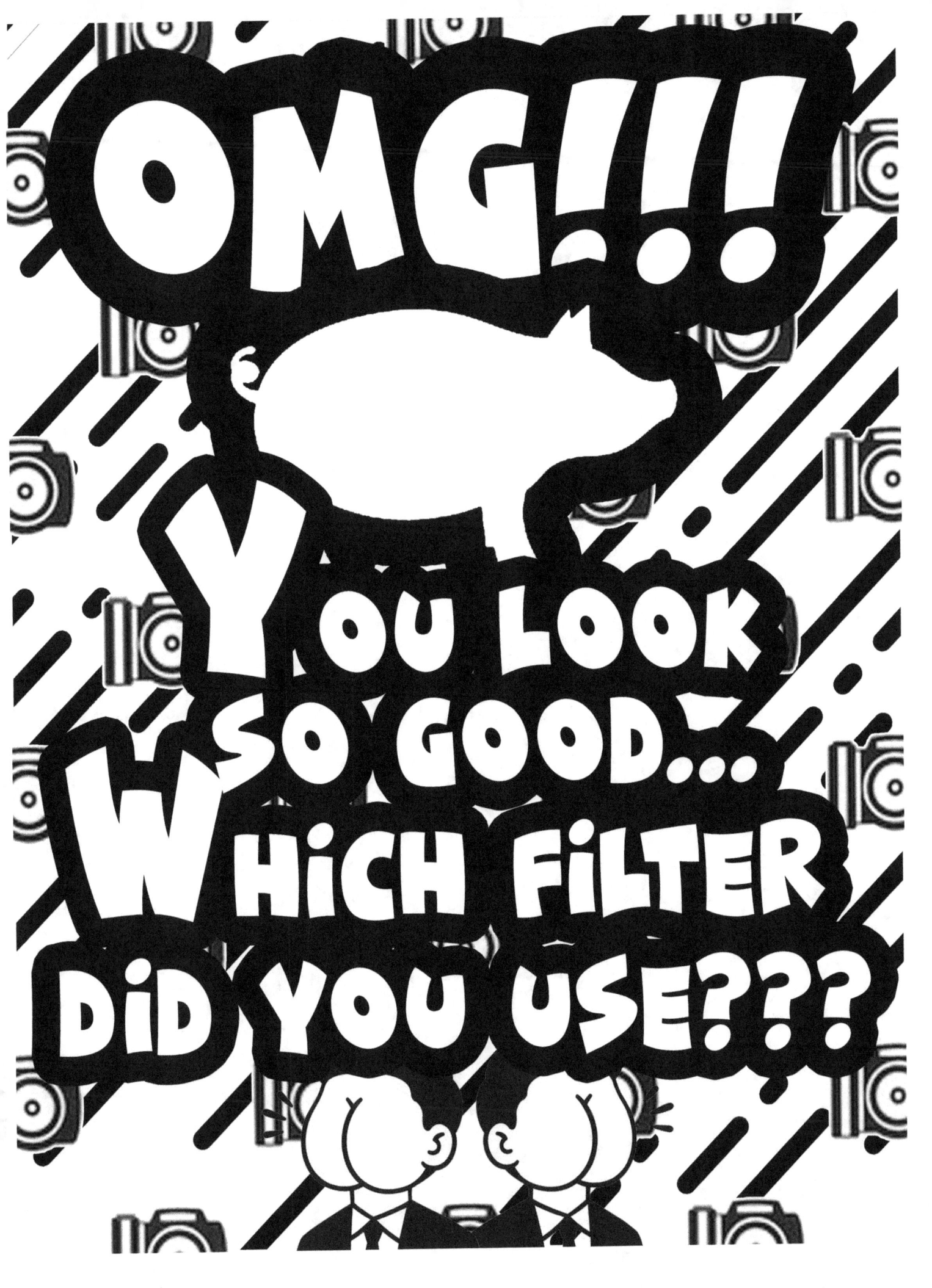

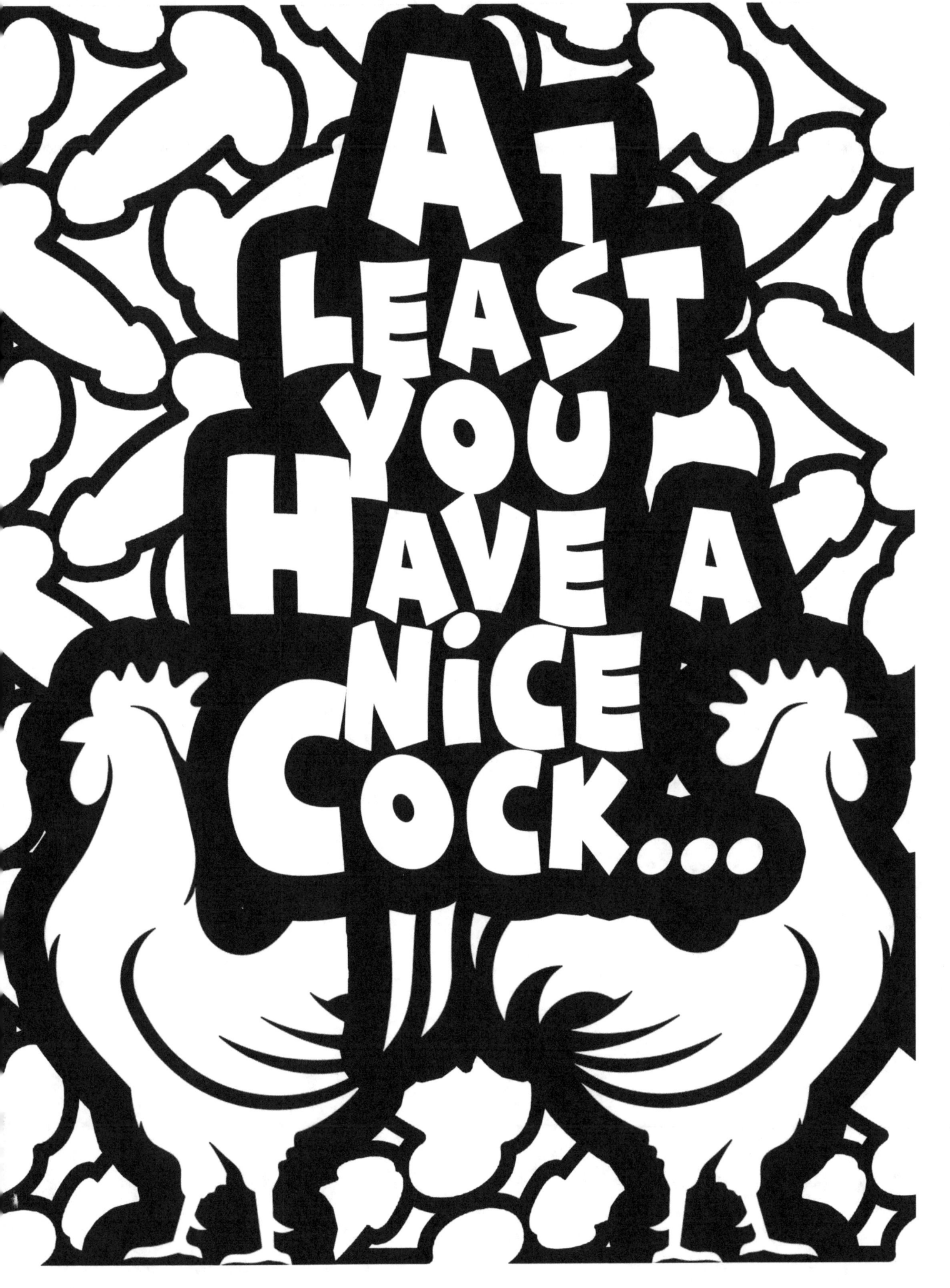

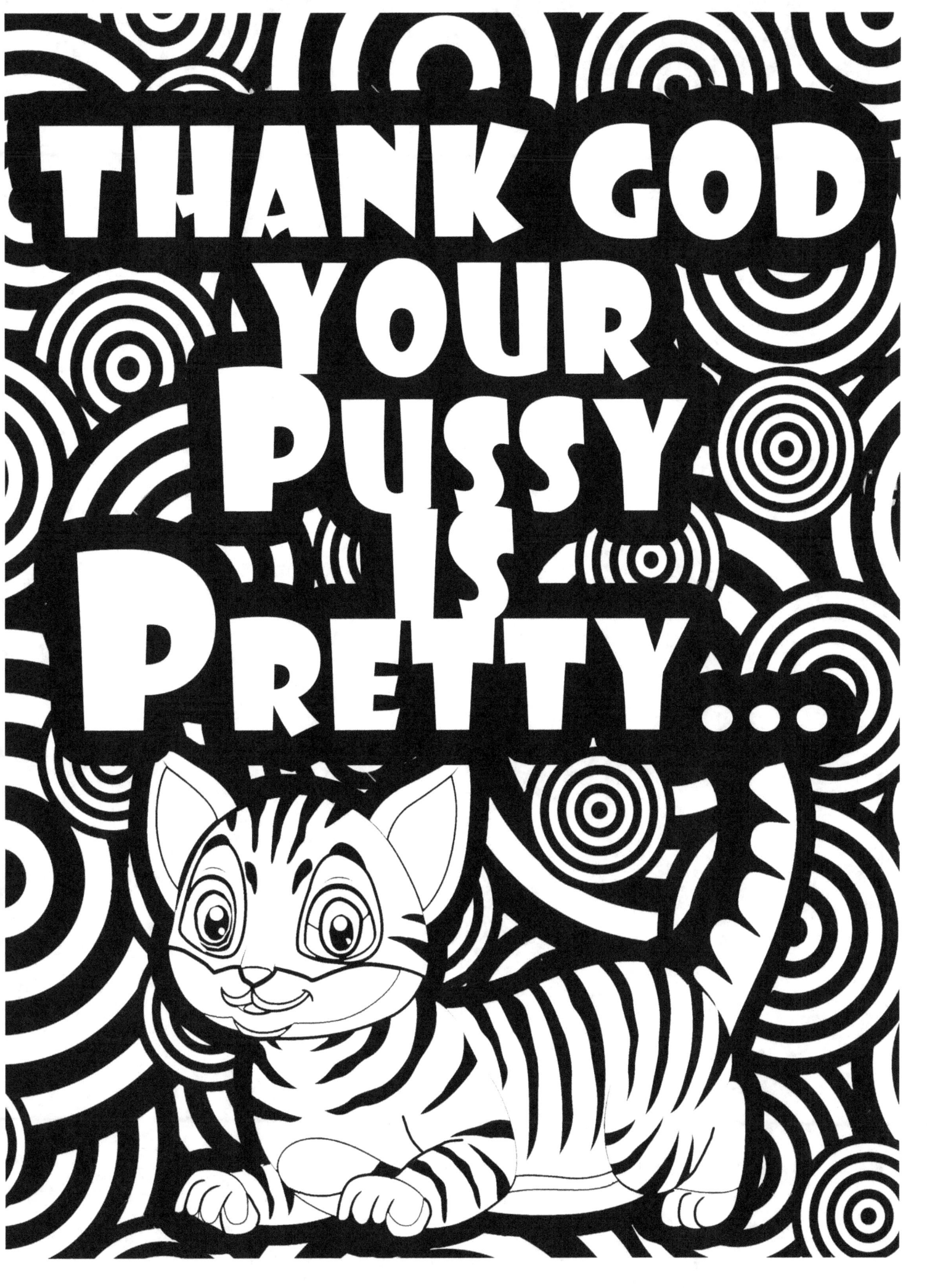

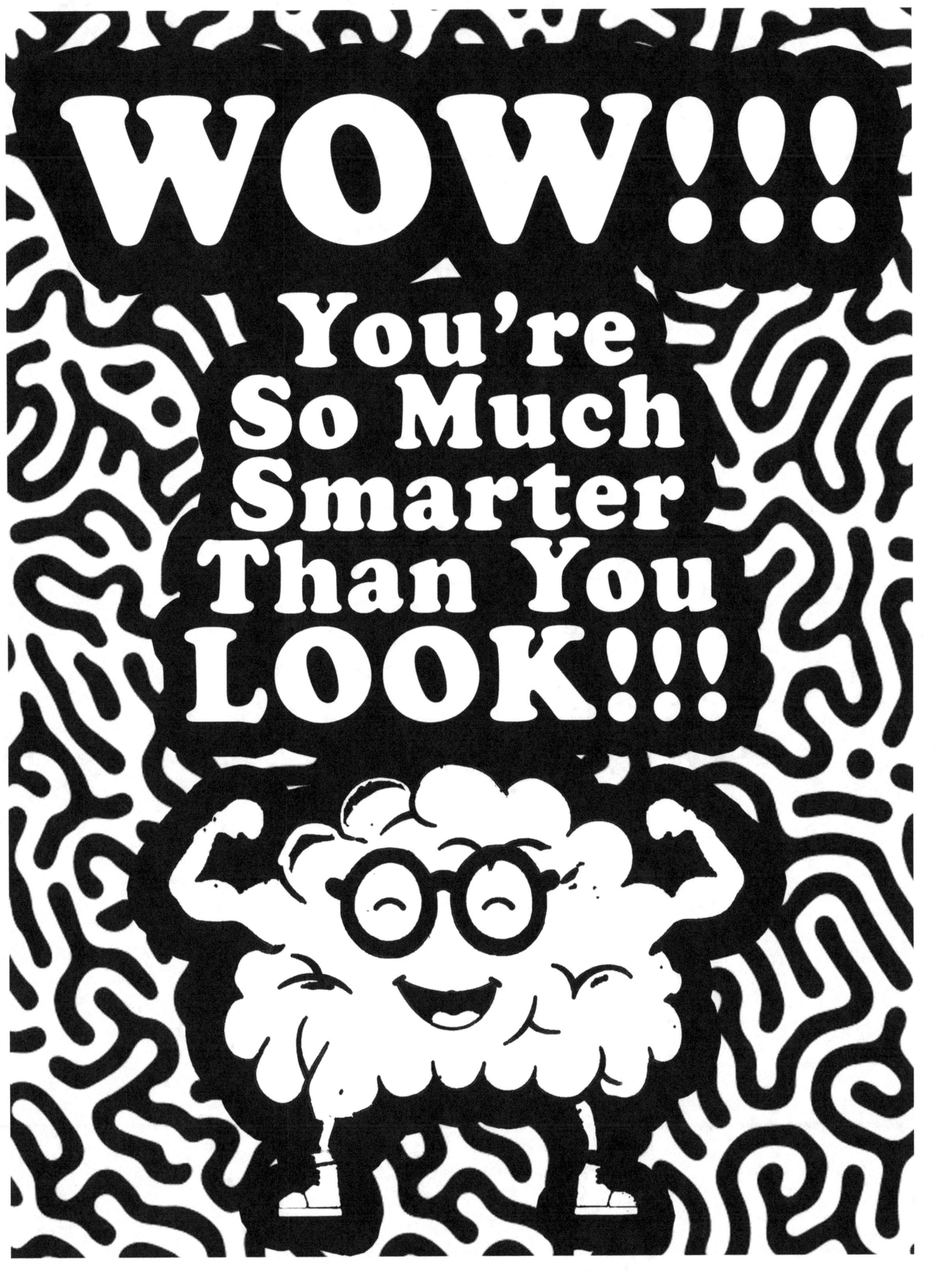

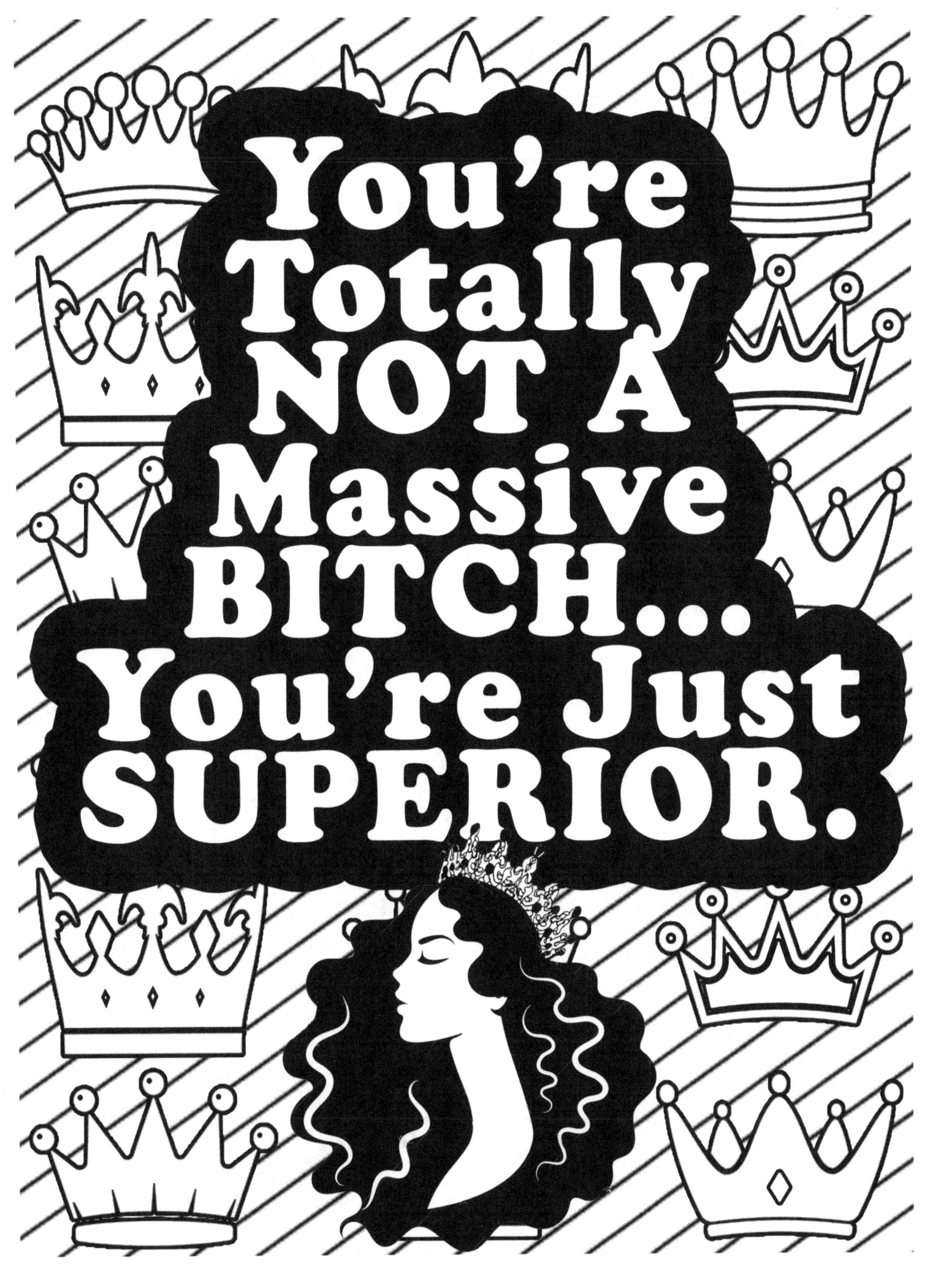

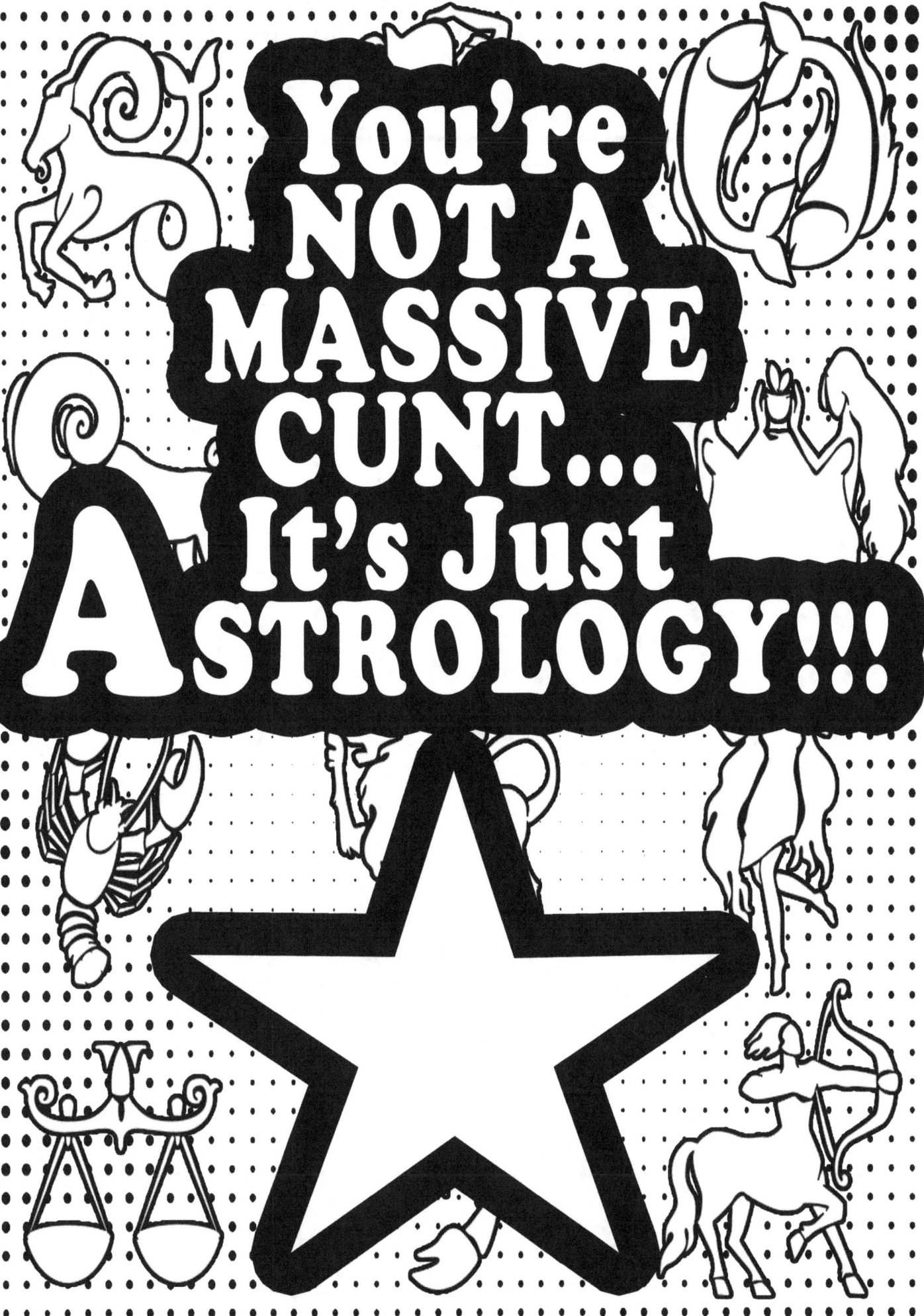

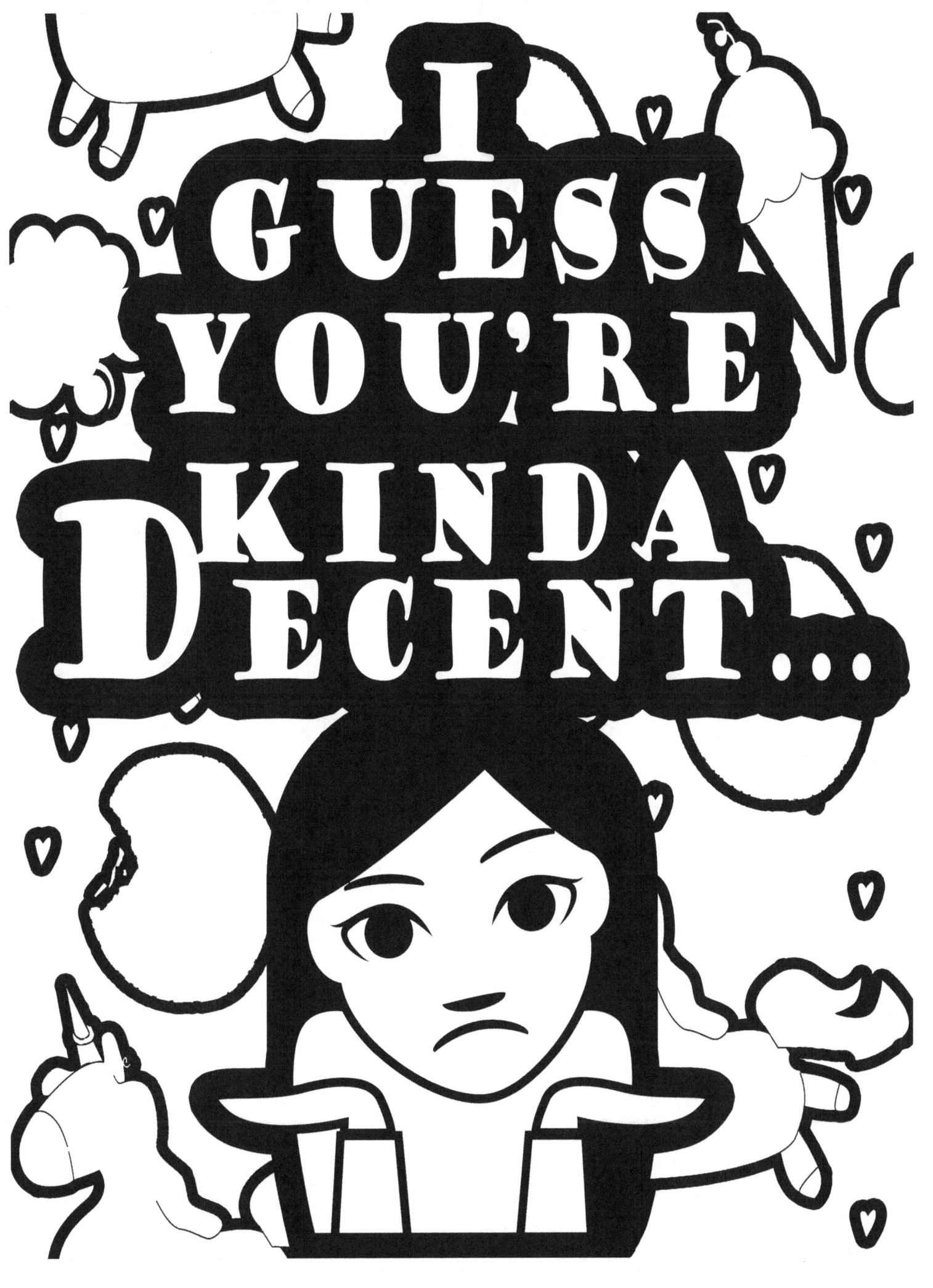

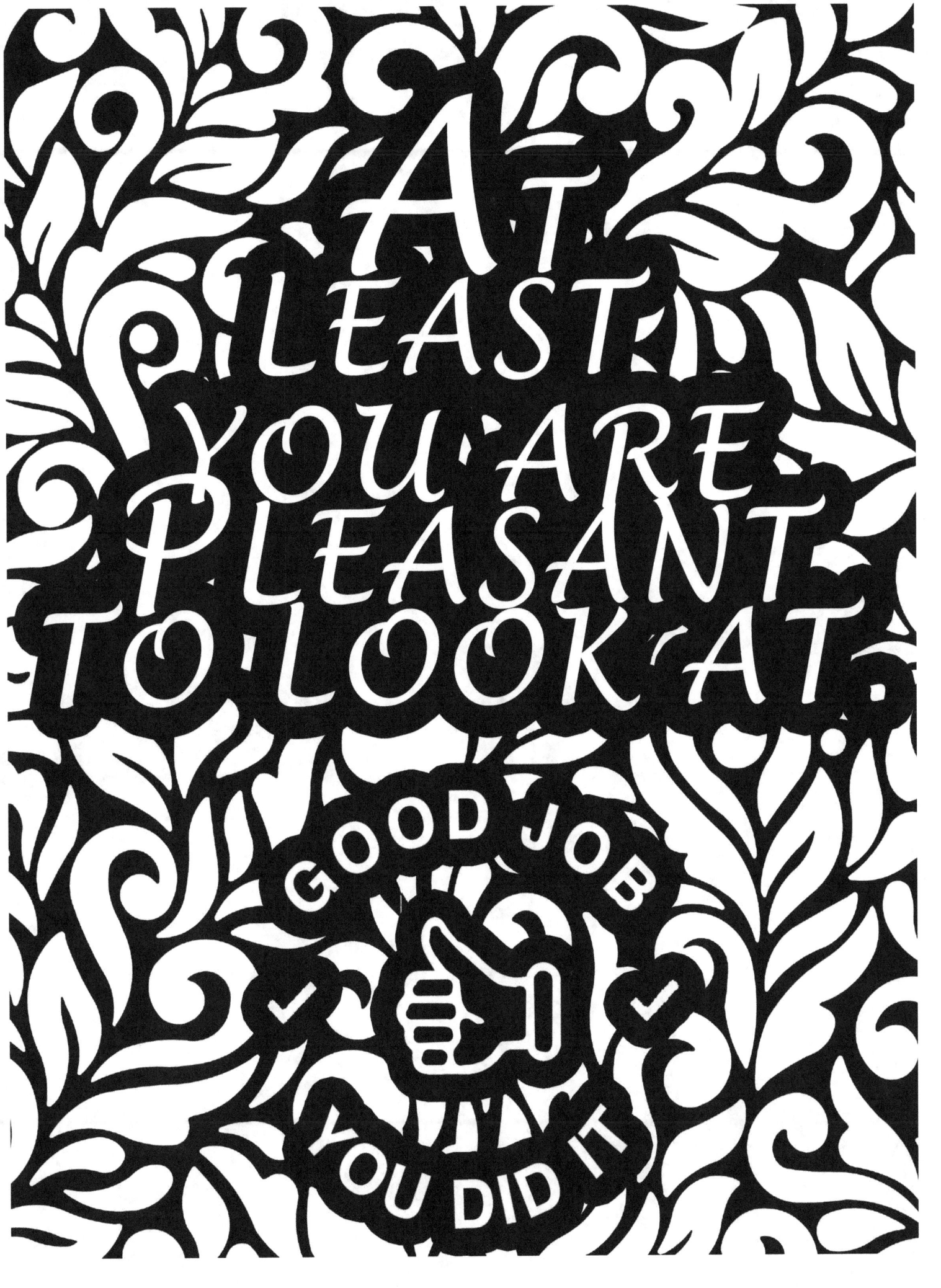

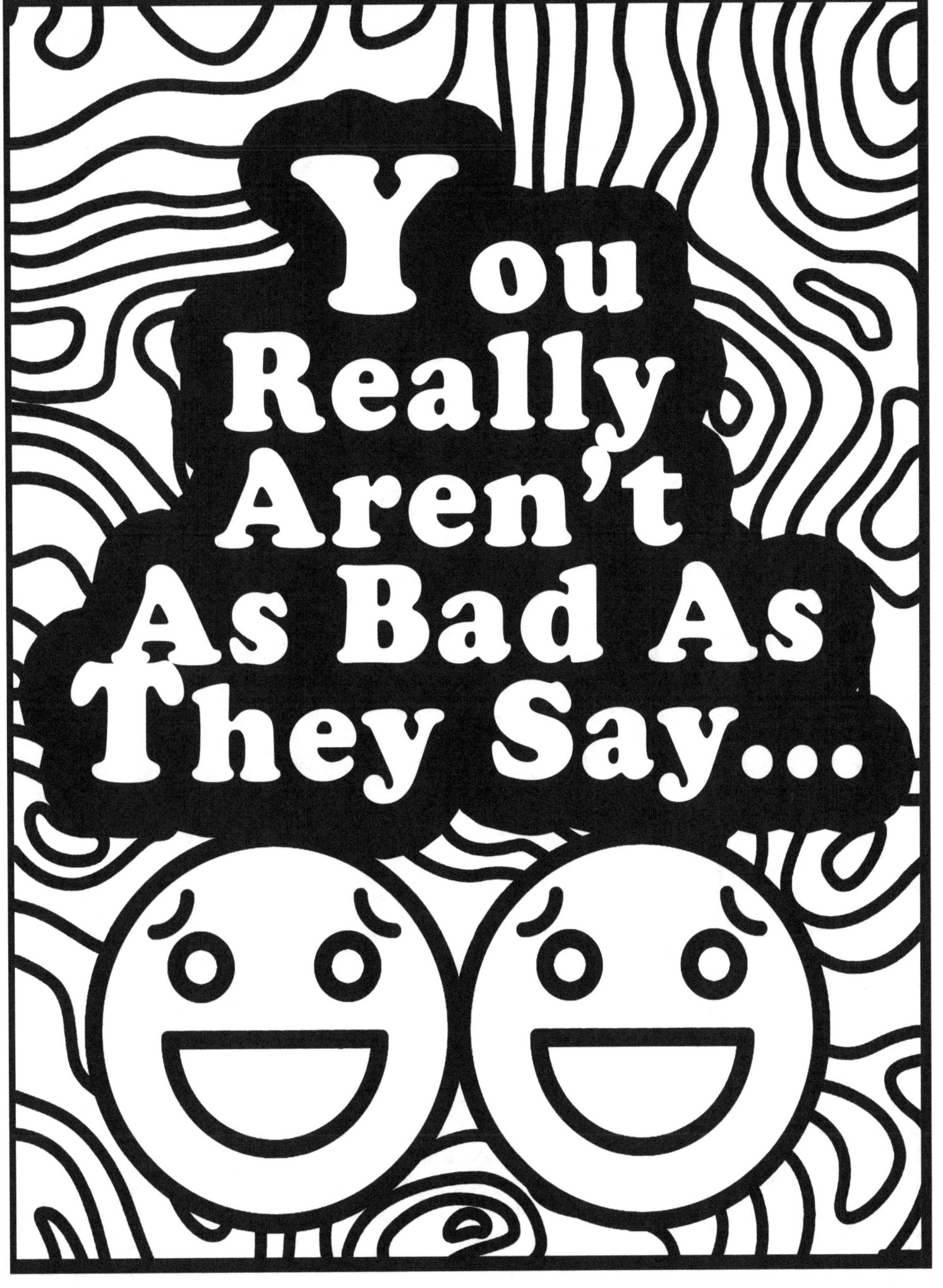

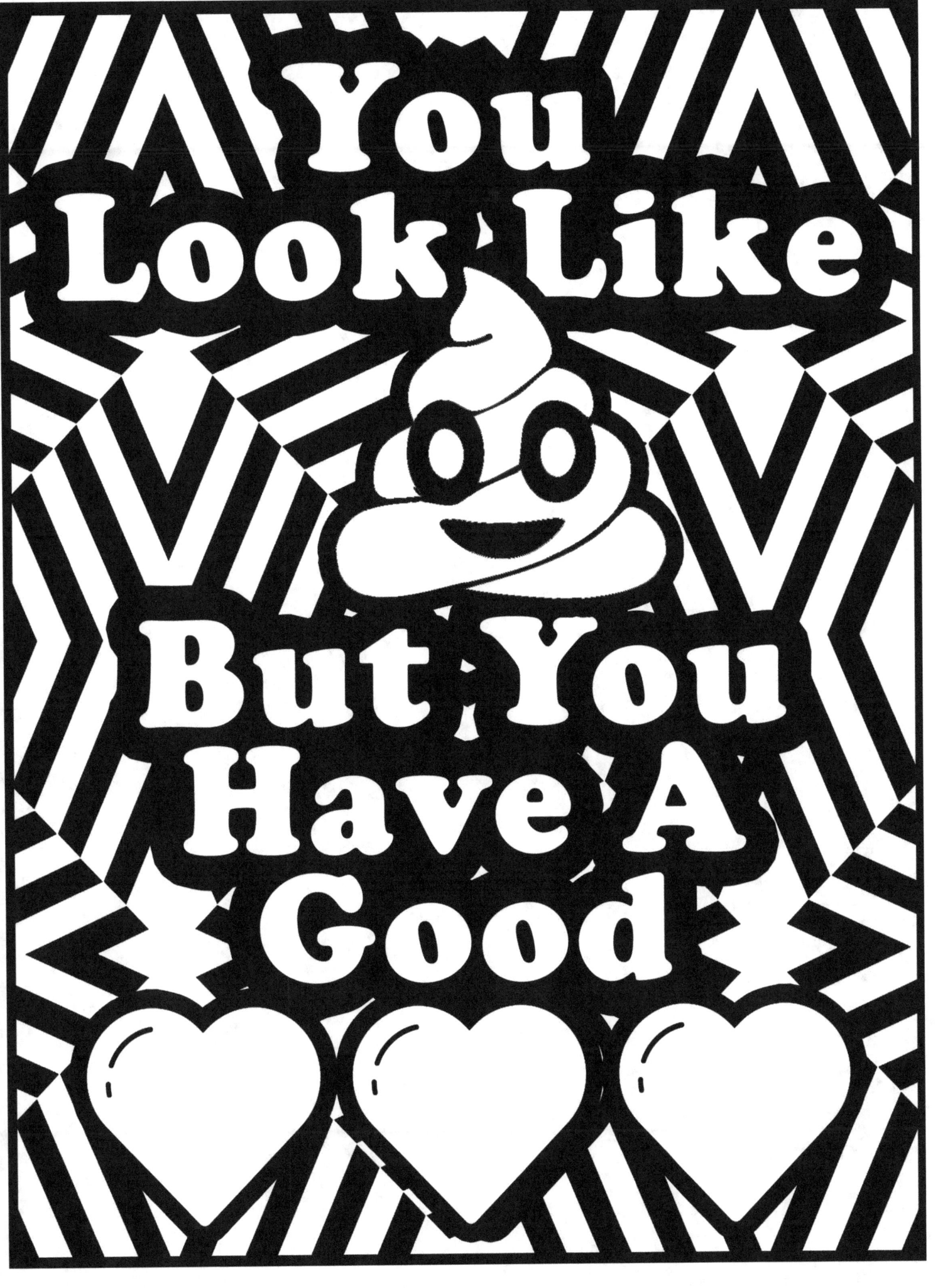

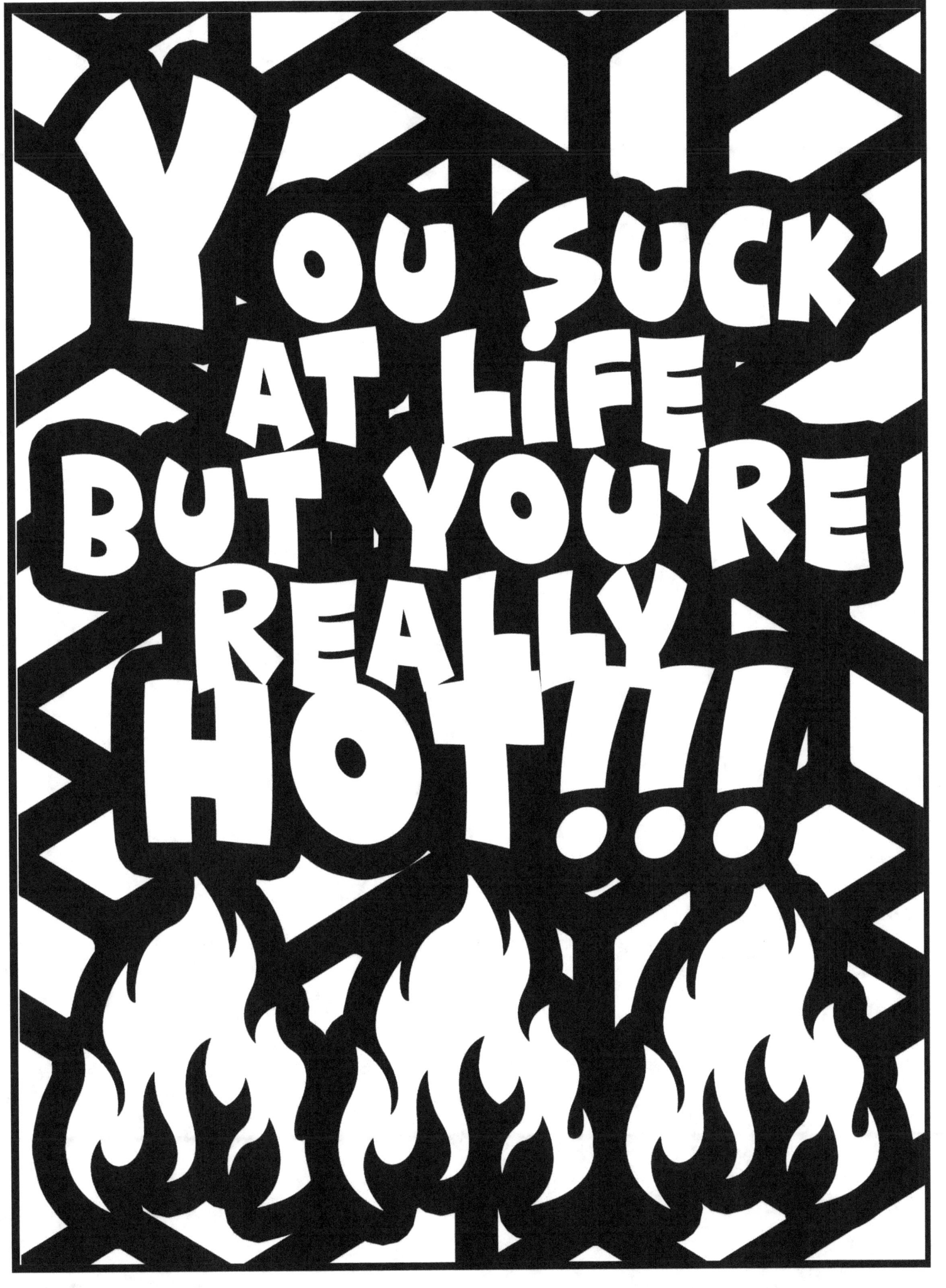

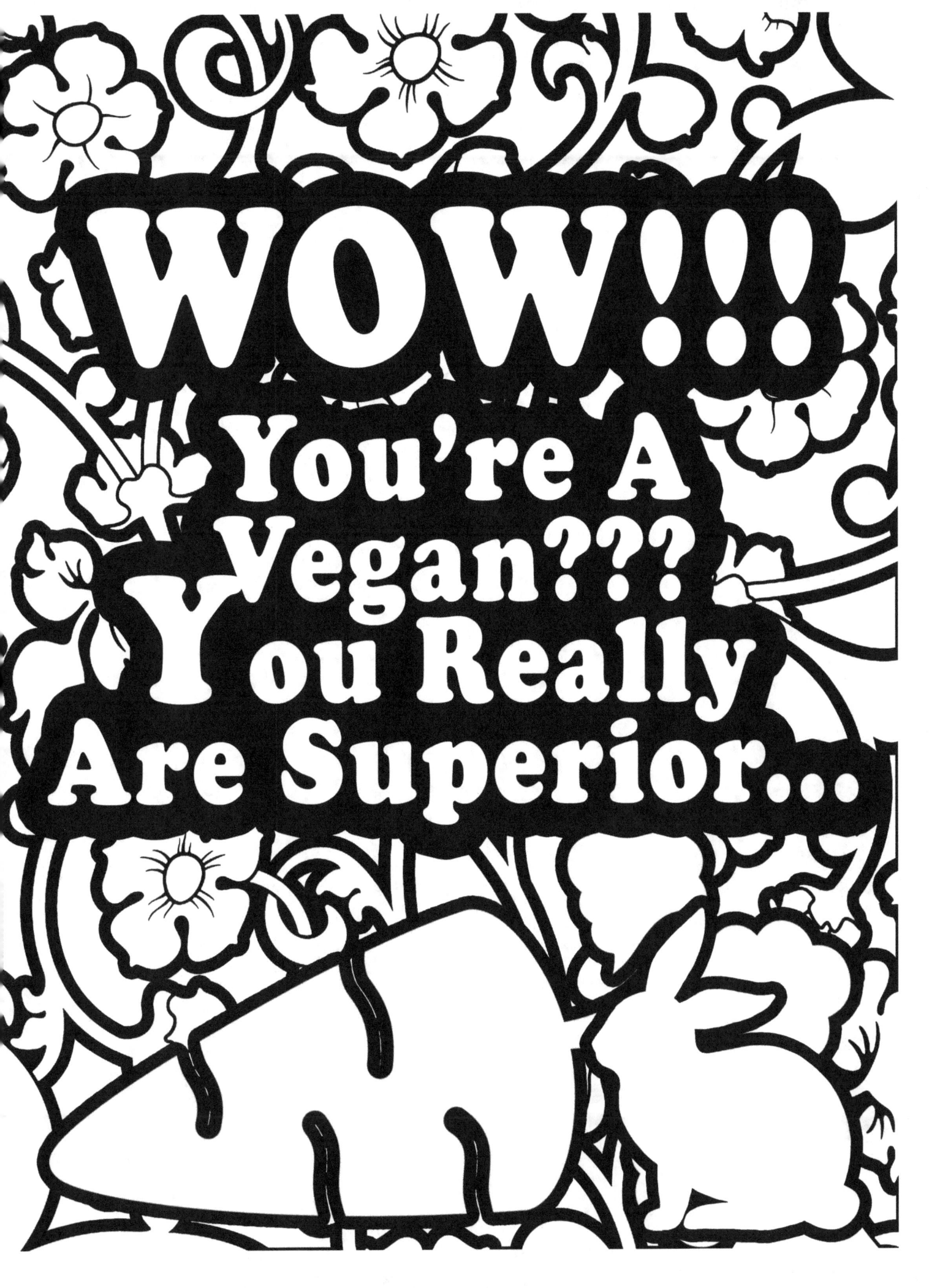

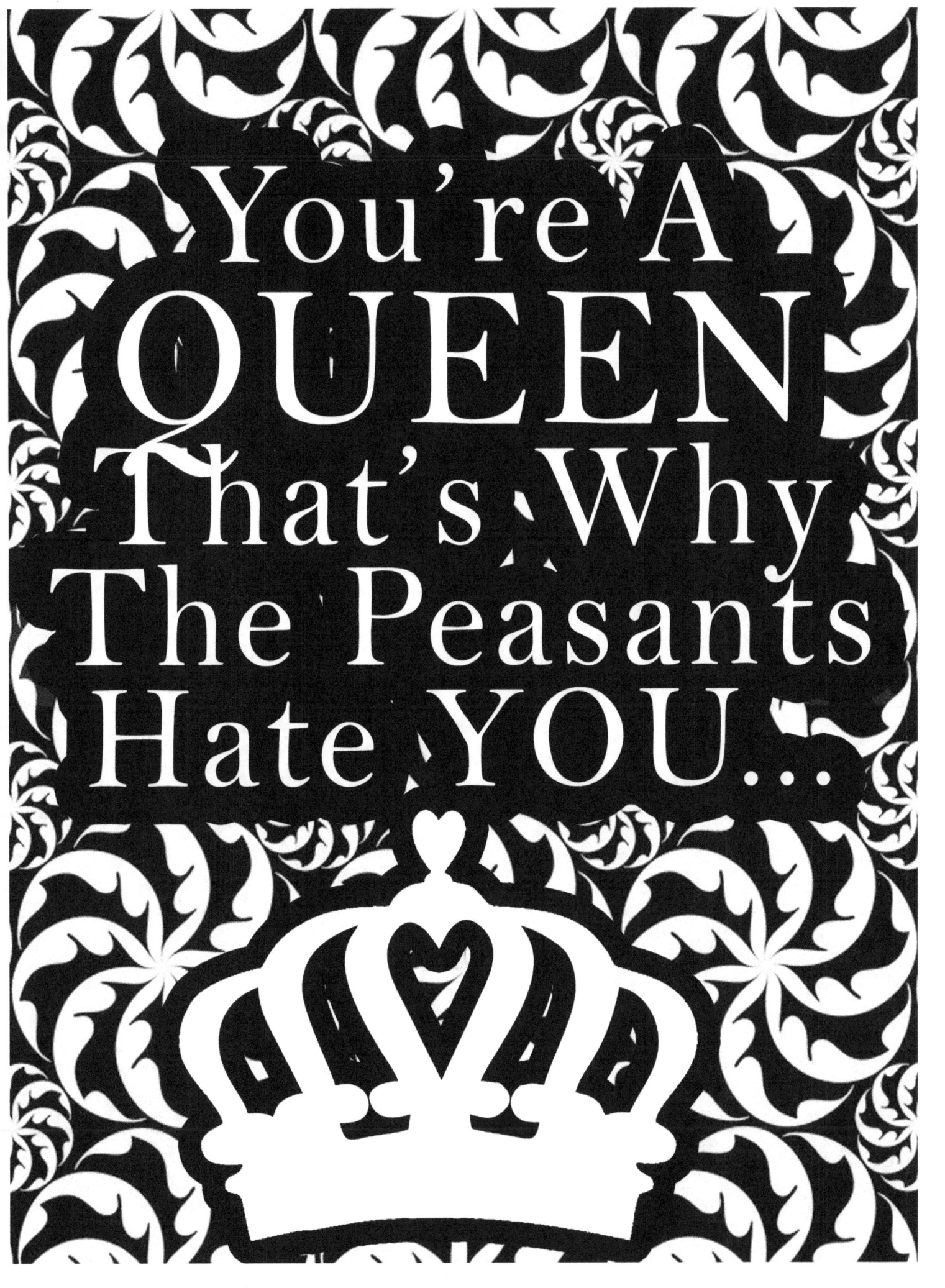

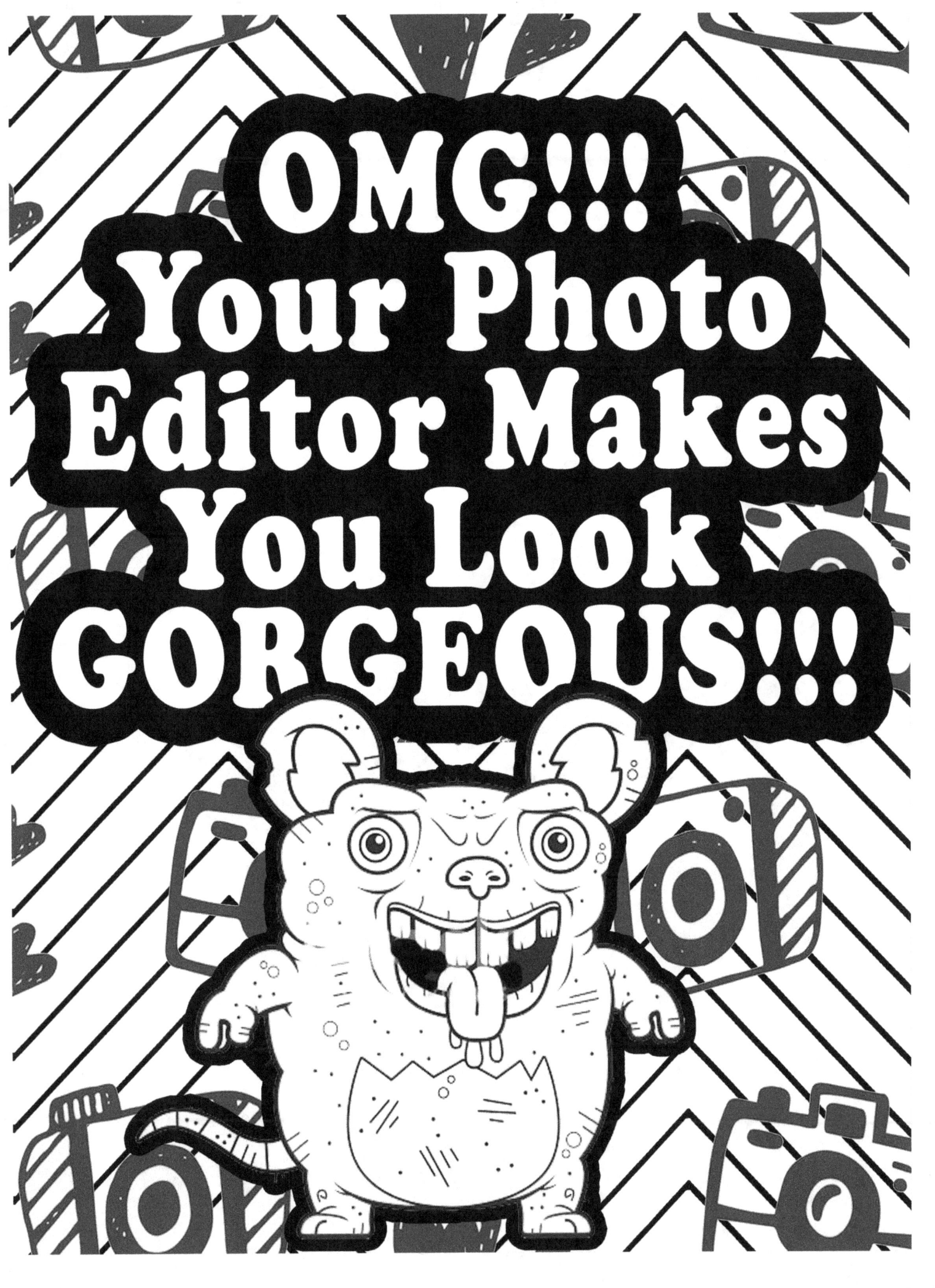

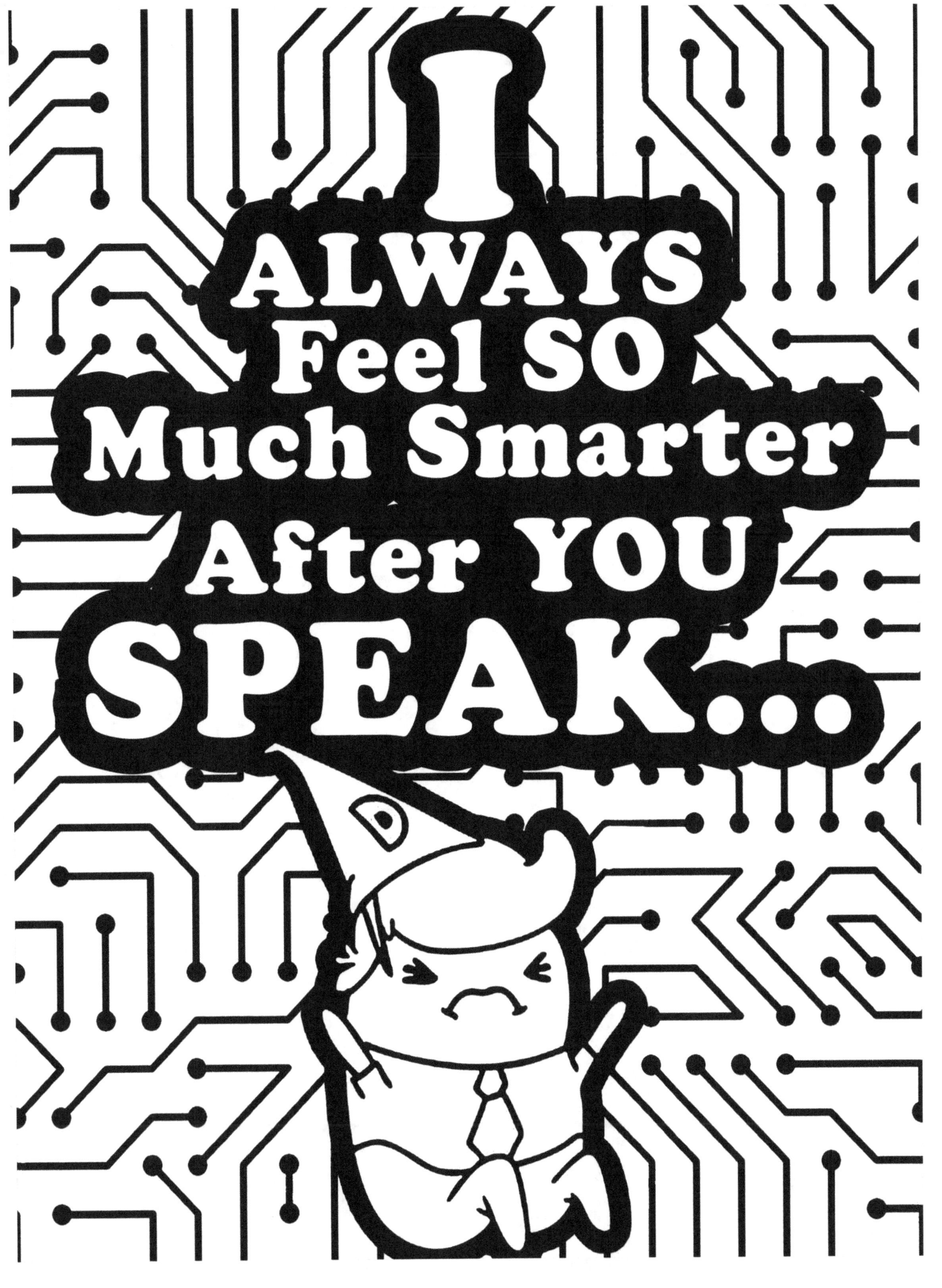

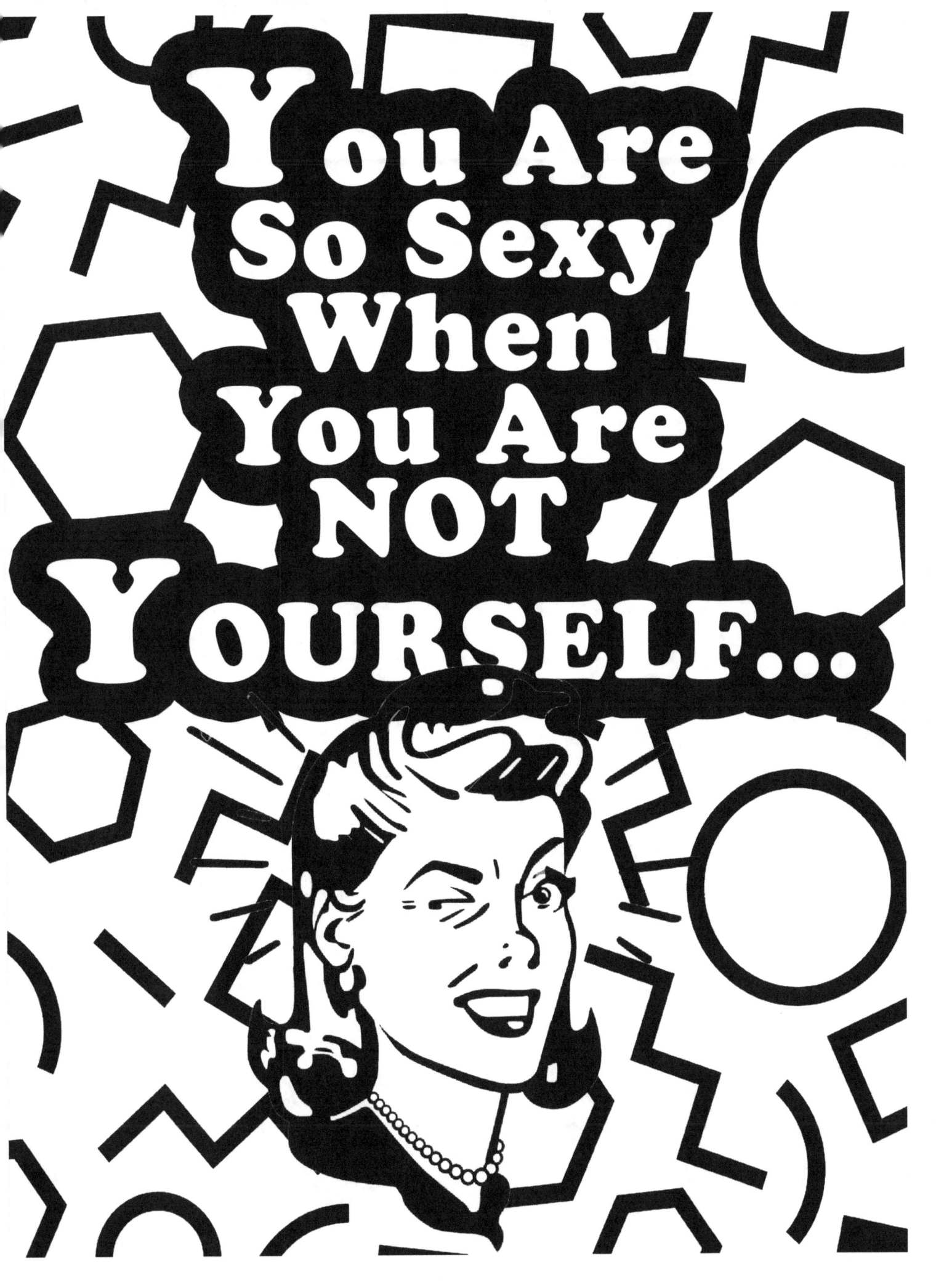

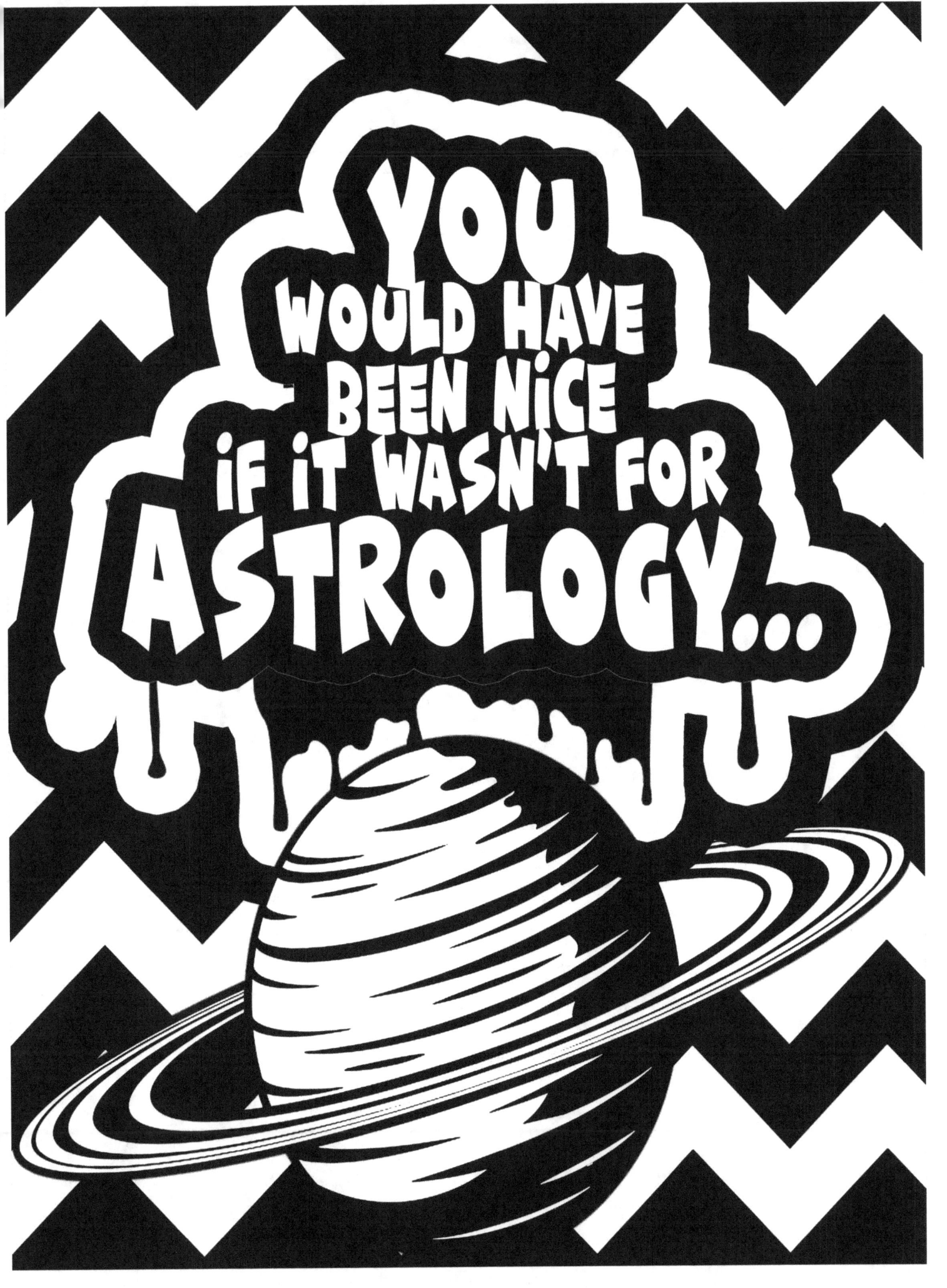

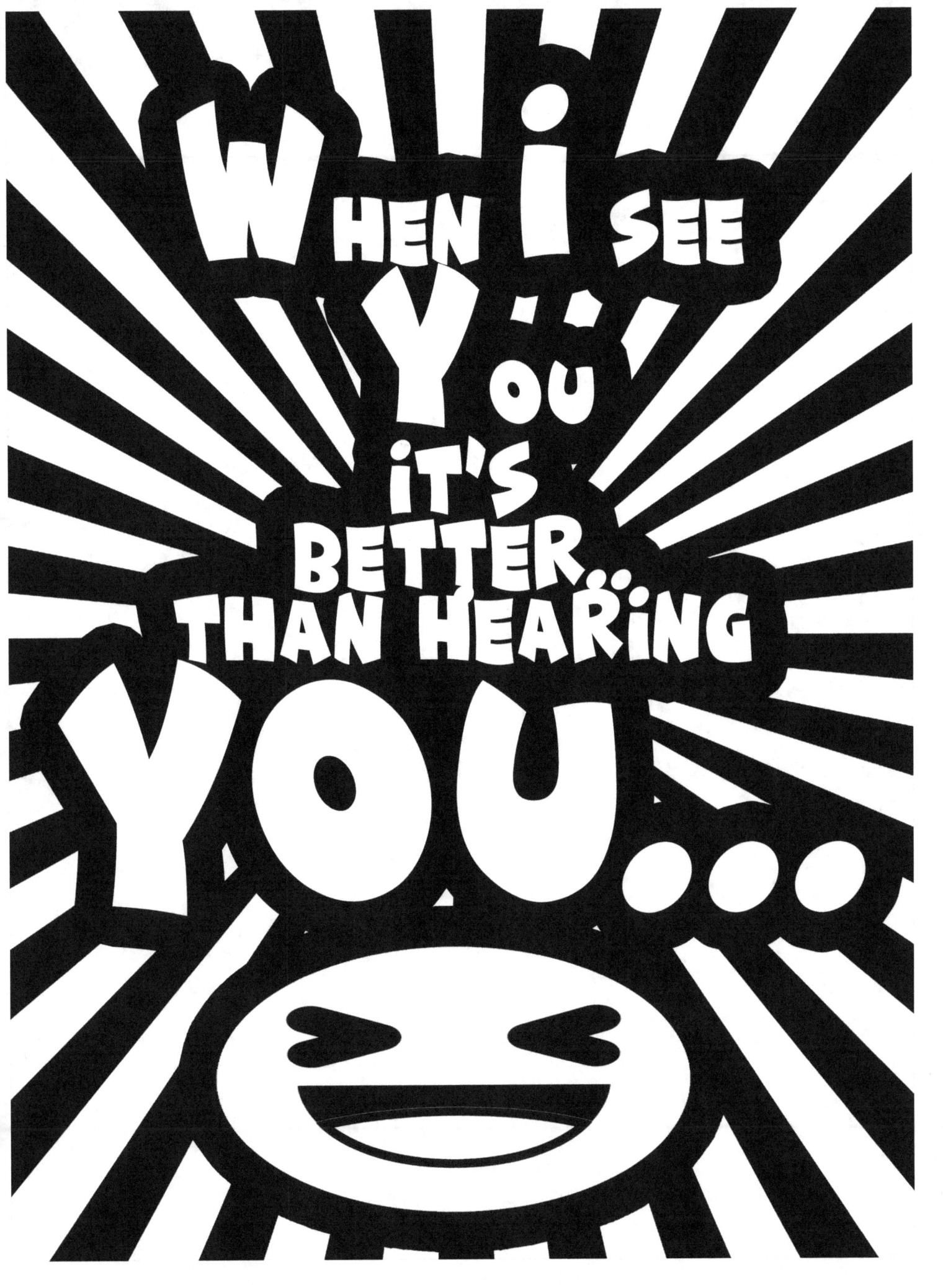

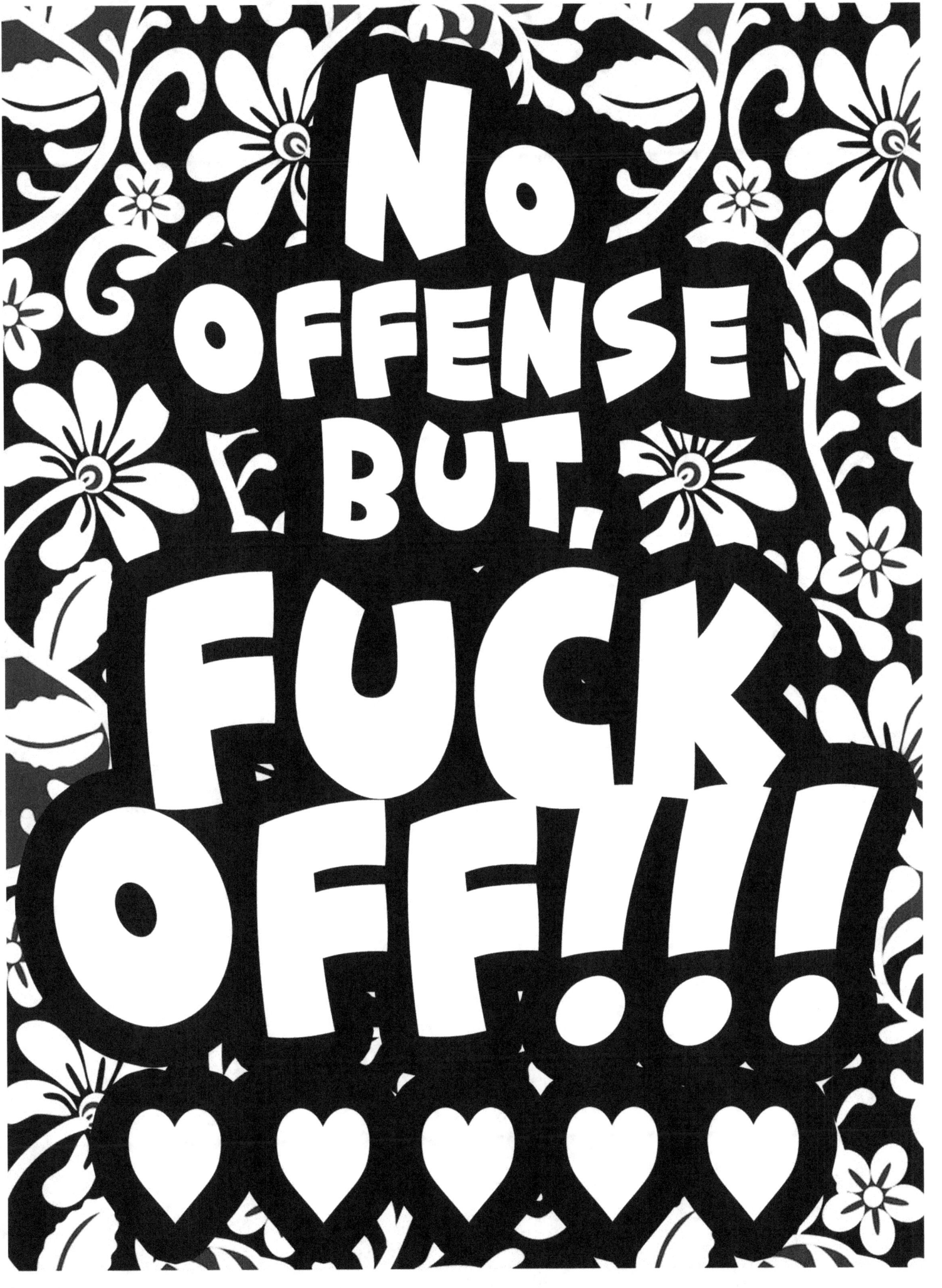

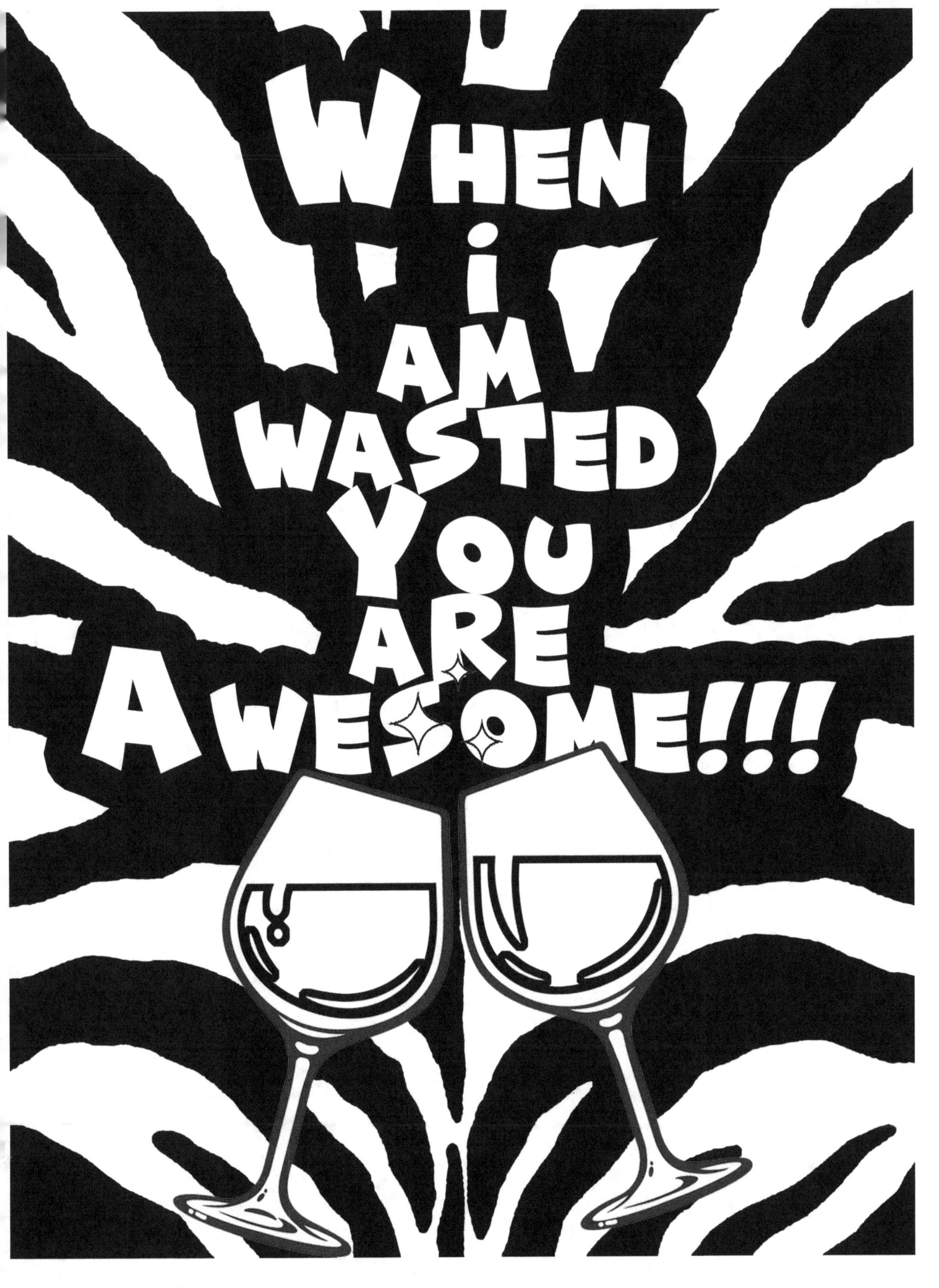

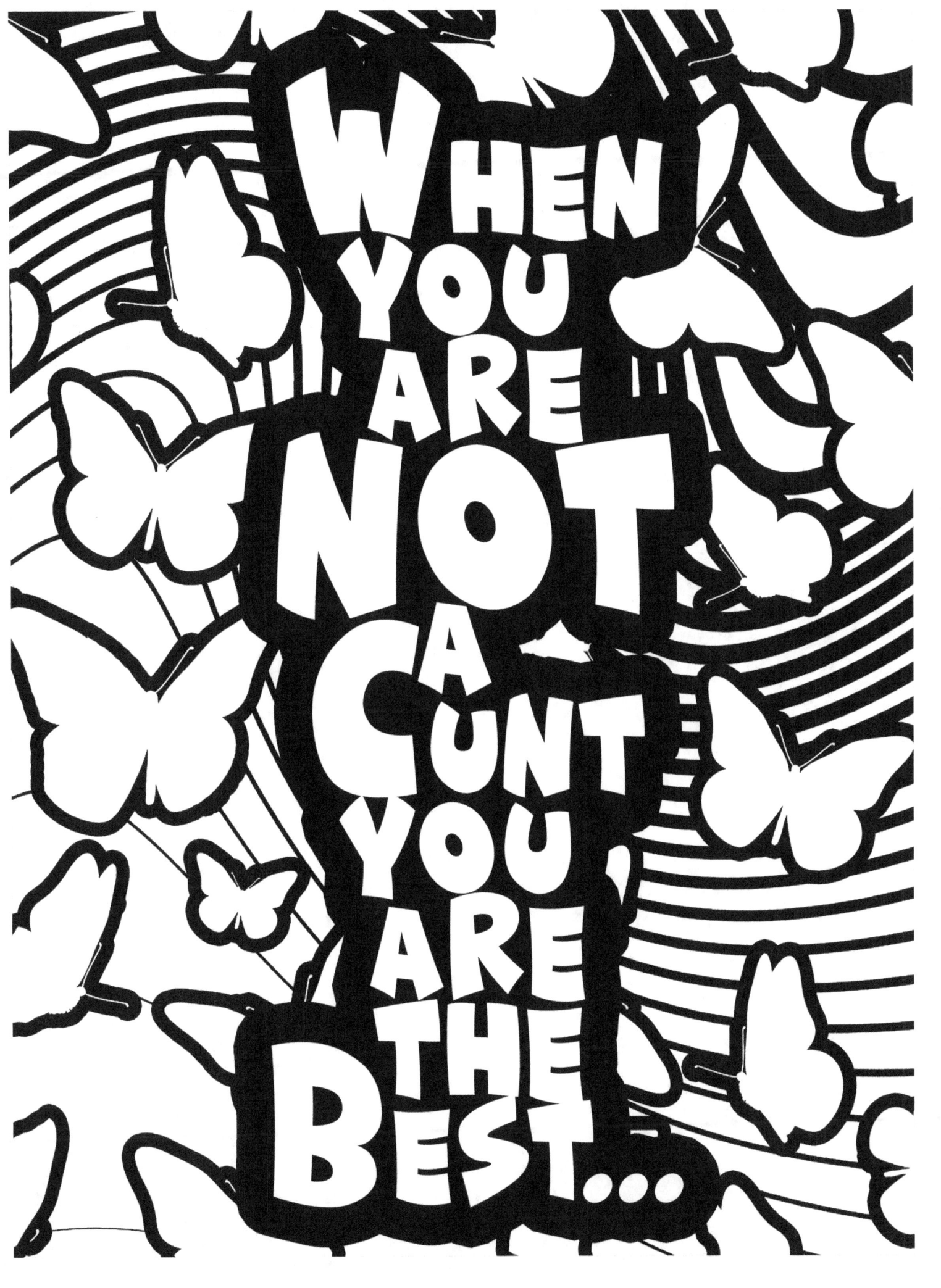

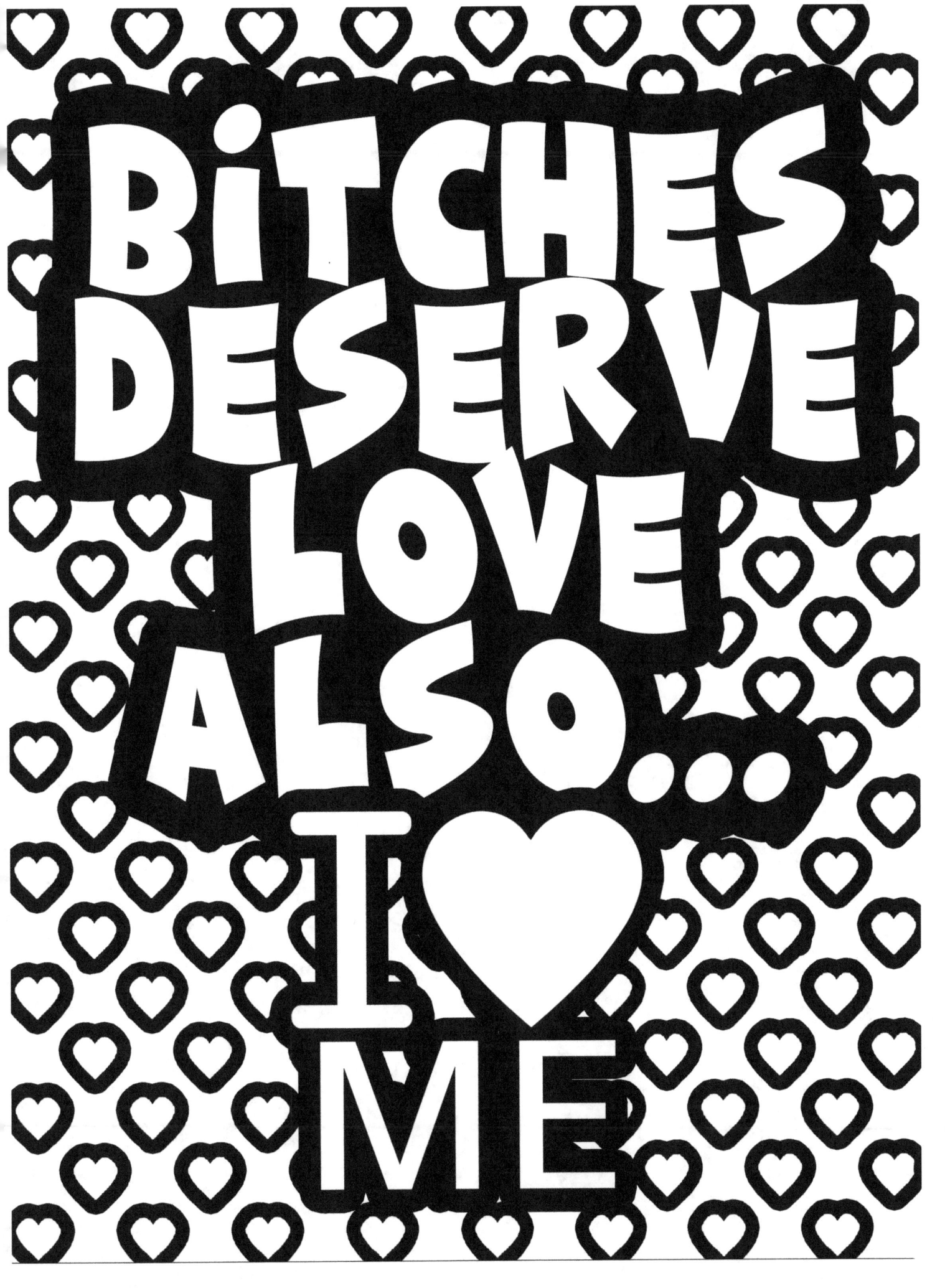

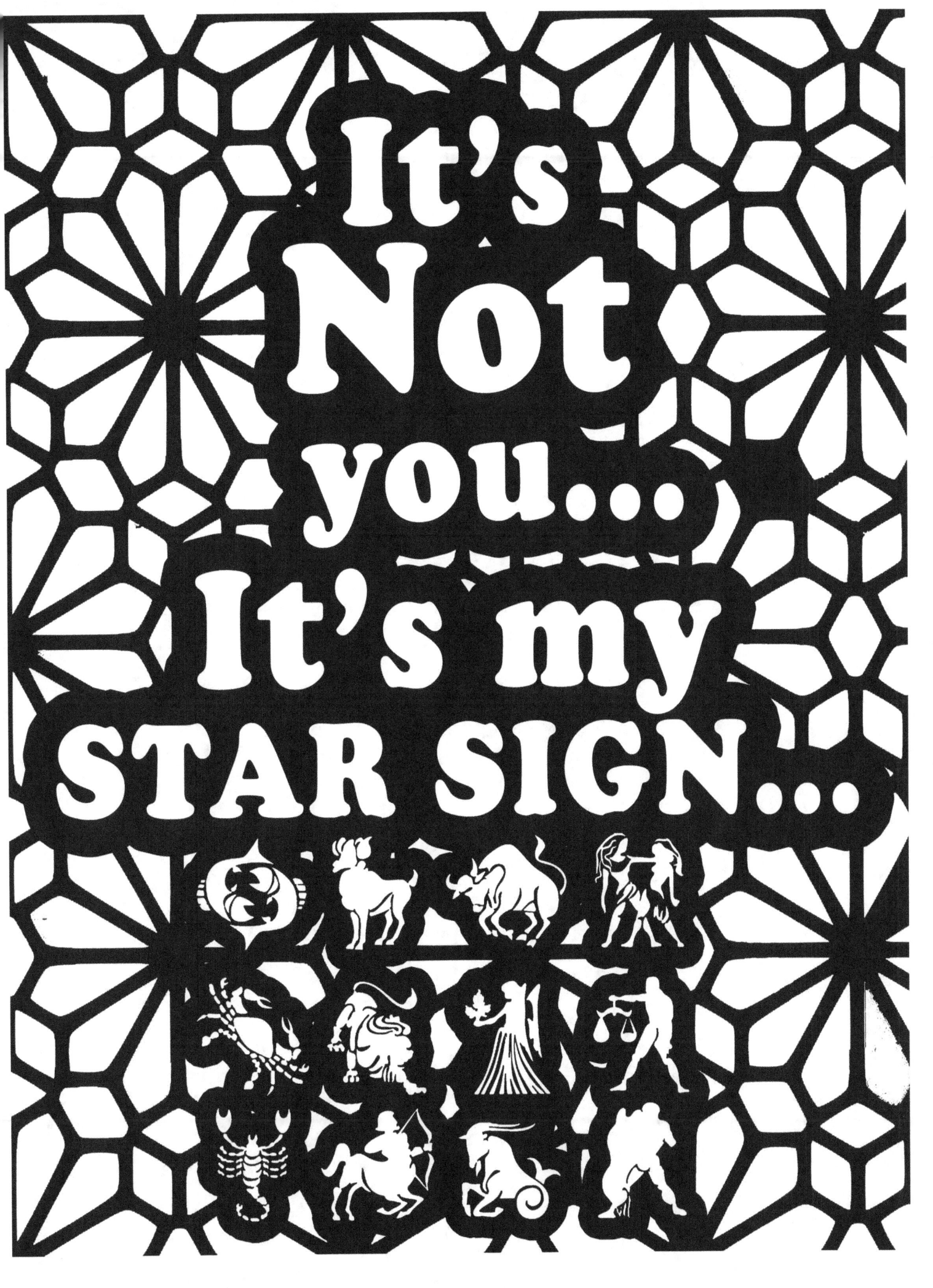

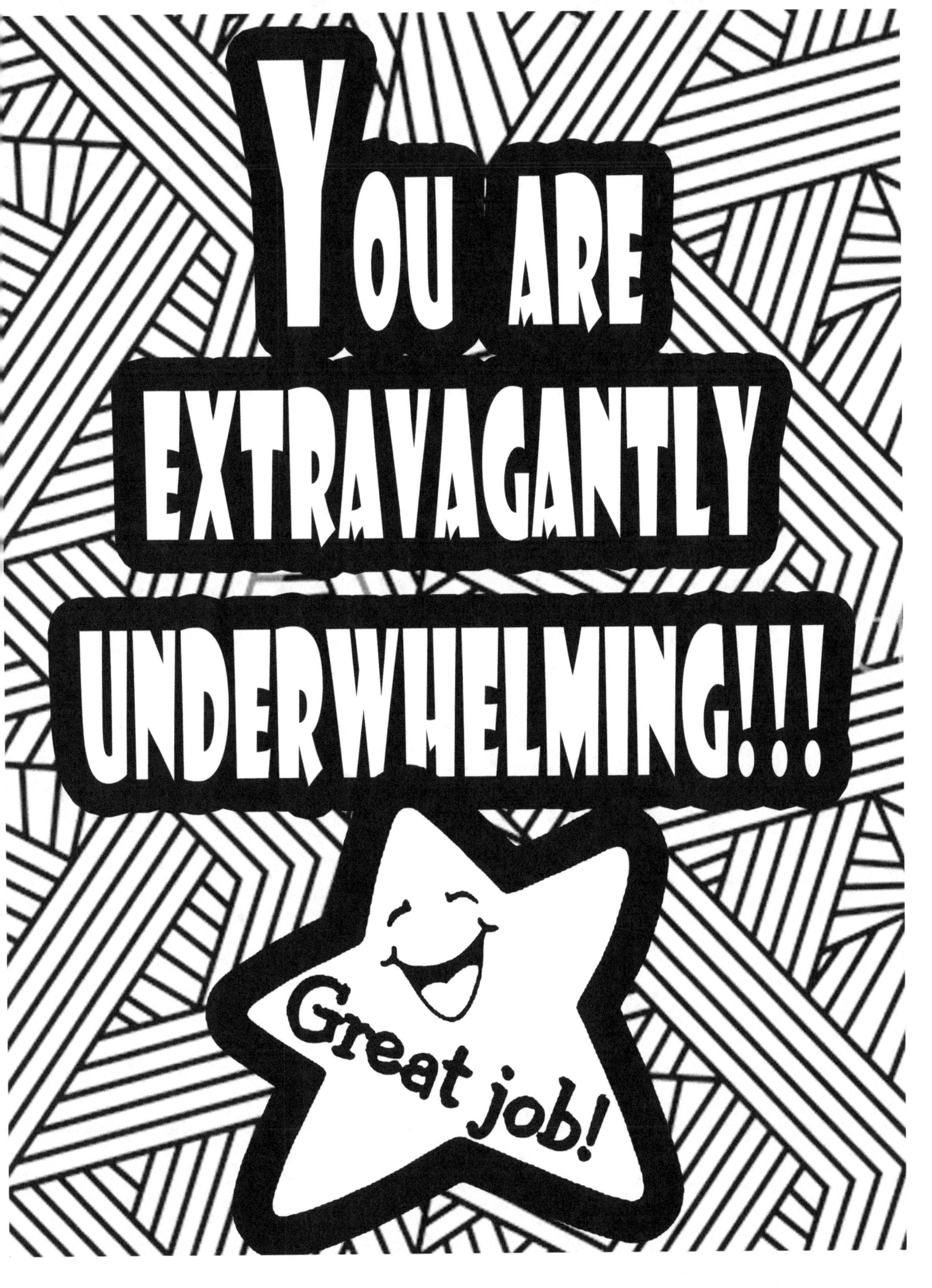

www.ingramcontent.com/pod-product-compliance
Lightning Source LLC
Chambersburg PA
CBHW080532220526
45465CB00006B/2681